Gypsy & Funny Girl

VOCAL SELECTIONS

Gypsy	Funny Girl
Music by JULE STYNE	Music by JULE STYNE
Lyrics by STEPHEN SONDHEIM	Lyrics by BOB MERRILL

CONTENTS

Project Manager: SY FELDMAN
Cover Design: JOE KLUCAR

WARNER BROS. PUBLICATIONS - THE GLOBAL LEADER IN PRINT
USA: 15800 NW 48th Avenue, Miami, FL 33014

WARNER/CHAPPELL MUSIC

CANADA: 15800 N.W. 48th AVENUE
MIAMI, FLORIDA 33014
SCANDINAVIA: P.O. BOX 533, VENDEVAGEN 85 B
S-182 15, DANDERYD, SWEDEN
AUSTRALIA: P.O. BOX 353
3 TALAVERA ROAD, NORTH RYDE N.S.W. 2113
ASIA: UNIT 901 - LIPPO SUN PLAZA
28 CANTON ROAD
TSIM SHA TSUI, KOWLOON, HONG KONG

NUOVA CARISCH

ITALY: VIA CAMPANIA, 12
20098 S. GIULIANO MILANESE (MI)
ZONA INDUSTRIALE SESTO ULTERIANO
SPAIN: MAGALLANES, 25
28015 MADRID
FRANCE: CARISCH MUSICOM,
25, RUE D'HAUTEVILLE, 75010 PARIS

INTERNATIONAL MUSIC PUBLICATIONS LIMITED

ENGLAND: GRIFFIN HOUSE,
161 HAMMERSMITH ROAD, LONDON W6 8BS
GERMANY: MARSTALLSTR. 8, D-80539 MUNCHEN
DENMARK: DANMUSIK, VOGNMAGERGADE 7
DK 1120 KOBENHAVNK

ALL I NEED IS THE GIRL

Words by
STEPHEN SONDHEIM

Music by
JULE STYNE

All I Need Is The Girl - 3 - 1

4

EVERYTHING'S COMING UP ROSES

Words by
STEPHEN SONDHEIM

Music by
JULE STYNE

Everything's Coming up Roses - 6 - 1

8

LET ME ENTERTAIN YOU

Words by
STEPHEN SONDHEIM

Music by
JULE STYNE

Let Me Entertain You - 3 - 1

12

Let Me Entertain You - 3 - 2

LITTLE LAMB

Words by
STEPHEN SONDHEIM

Music by
JULE STYNE

Little Lamb - 3 - 1

SMALL WORLD

Lyrics by
STEPHEN SONDHEIM

Music by
JULE STYNE

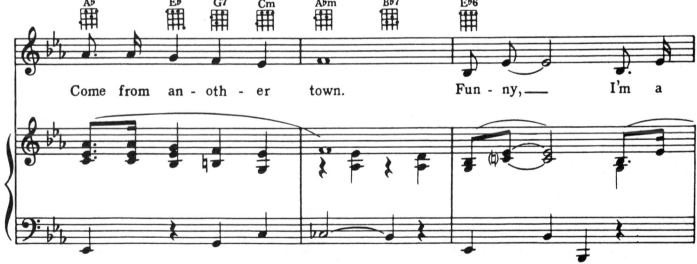

Small World - 4 - 1

Small World - 4 - 2

SOME PEOPLE

Words by
STEPHEN SONDHEIM

Music by
JULE STYNE

Some People - 5 - 1

22

don't know____ they're a - live._____

Some peo - ple can thrive and bloom ____

Liv - ing life ____ in a liv - ing room.____

That's per - fect for some peo - ple of

Some People - 5 - 2

one hun - dred and five _____ But

I _____ at least ____ got - ta

try, _____ When I ____ think of

all the sights that I ____ got - ta see yet, All the plac - es I ____

24

TOGETHER WHEREVER WE GO

Words by
STEPHEN SONDHEIM

Music by
JULE STYNE

Together Wherever We Go - 4 - 1

Together Wherever We Go - 4 - 4

YOU'LL NEVER GET AWAY FROM ME

Lyrics by
STEPHEN SONDHEIM

Music by
JULE STYNE

You'll never get away from me,
You can climb the tallest tree, I'll be there somehow.
True,

You'll Never Get Away From Me - 3 - 1

You'll Never Get Away From Me - 3 - 2

FUNNY GIRL

Words by
BOB MERRILL

Music by
JULE STYNE

Funny Girl - 3 - 1

34

Funny Girl - 3 - 2

SADIE, SADIE

Words by
BOB MERRILL

Music by
JULE STYNE

Sadie, Sadie - 3 - 1

Sadie, Sadie - 3 - 3

I'M THE GREATEST STAR

Words by
BOB MERRILL

Music by
JULE STYNE

In The Greatest Star - 4 - 1

YOU ARE WOMAN, I AM MAN

Words by
BOB MERRILL

Music by
JULE STYNE

You Are Woman, I Am Man - 3 - 1

I AM WOMAN, YOU ARE MAN
(Female Version)

1st Chorus

I am woman, you are man.

I am smaller, so you can be taller than.

You are softer to the touch.

It's a feeling I like feeling very much.

You are someone I've admired.

Still our friendship leaves something to be desired.

Does it take more explanation than this?

I am woman, you are man.

I am woman, you are man, let's kiss.

2nd Chorus

I am woman, you are man.

I am gentle, you are barbarian.

I am pleats and pins and rouge.

Mostly sham but man, I love the subterfuge.

I am fiction, you are fact.

Contradiction's what makes it a perfect act.

Does it take more explanation than this?

I am woman, you are man.

I am woman, you are man, let's kiss.

DON'T RAIN ON MY PARADE

Words by
BOB MERRILL

Music by
JULE STYNE

Don't Rain On My Parade - 8 - 1

48

(may be played octave lower)

Don't Rain On My Parade - 8 - 2

50

Don't Rain On My Parade - 8 - 5

52

54

Don't Rain On My Parade - 8 - 8

HIS LOVE MAKES ME BEAUTIFUL

Words by
BOB MERRILL

Music by
JULE STYNE

Here comes the bride, A - noth - er beau - ti - ful bride.

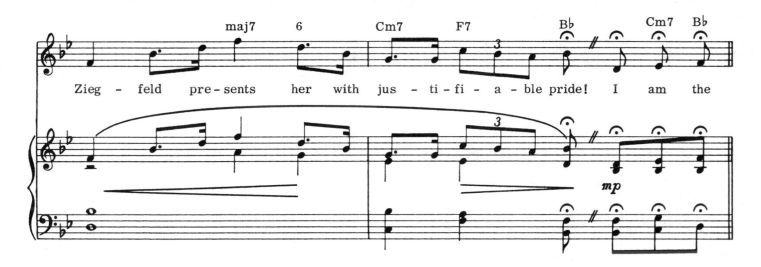

Zieg - feld pre - sents her with jus - ti - fi - a - ble pride! I am the

Refrain-Slowly

beau - ti - ful re - flec - tion Of my love's af - fec - tion, A

His Love Makes Me Beatiful - 3 - 1

56

His Love Makes Me Beatiful - 3 - 2

His Love Makes Me Beatiful - 3 - 3

PEOPLE

Words by
BOB MERRILL

Music by
JULE STYNE

People - 3 - 1

60

People - 3 - 3